TERRITORIES

© Aladdin Books 1991

All rights reserved

Designed and produced by
Aladdin Books Ltd
28 Percy Street
London W1P 9FF

*First published in 1991
in Great Britain by*
Franklin Watts Ltd
96 Leonard Street
London EC2A 4RH

A CIP catalogue record
for this book is
available from the
British Library.

ISBN: 0 7496 0694 0

Printed in Belgium

Terry Jennings is an author
who has produced more than
100 books for children
on science, geography
and natural history.

Steve Parker is a writer and
editor in the life sciences,
health and medicine, who has
written more than 50 books for
children on science and nature.

Jane Parker has a degree in
zoology, has worked as a
researcher at London Zoo, and
now works as a publishing
researcher and indexer.

Design: David West
Children's Book Design
Designer: John Kelly
Editor: Jen Green
Picture researcher: Emma Krikler
Illustrator: Michael Taylor

Photocredits
Cover and all pages apart from
page 6 top and bottom, 12 left,
27 bottom and 29 are from
Bruce Coleman Limited; pages 6
top and 27 bottom: Planet Earth
Pictures; page 6 bottom:
Spectrum Colour Library; page
12 left: Zig
Leszczynski/Animals
Animals/Oxford Scientific
Films; page 29: Eye Ubiquitous.

ANIMAL BEHAVIOUR
TERRITORIES

TERRY JENNINGS
WITH
STEVE & JANE PARKER

GLOUCESTER PRESS
London · New York · Toronto · Sydney

CONTENTS

INTRODUCTION	5
WHY HAVE TERRITORIES?	6
DEFENDING A TERRITORY	8
MESSAGES AT A DISTANCE	10
FINDING ENOUGH FOOD	12
A PLACE TO REST	14
GROUP TERRITORY	16
STAGE SHOW	18
SUPPORTING A FAMILY	20
BOUNDARY CONFRONTATION	22
BIGGEST AND BEST-ARMED	24
RITUAL FIGHTING	26
THE BIG FIGHT	28
SPOT IT YOURSELF	30
GLOSSARY	31
INDEX	32

INTRODUCTION

A territory is a patch of land or place which an animal occupies, and defends against others of its species (and sometimes against members of other species, too). It is as though the animal "owns" that particular area.

Animal behaviour is aimed at survival. For an individual animal to survive, it needs to eat and to avoid being eaten. And for a whole animal species to survive, some of its members must breed, so their kind is reproduced.

Territories, and the many types of behaviour that go with them, are connected with these fundamental concerns: with finding enough food, with breeding, or with both. A territory may also provide a safe place for an animal to rest or sleep.

Private property
Many, many animals use territories, and scientists are finding more all the time. Some territories are hundreds of kilometres across, others are only slightly bigger than the "owner". Some are occupied all the time, others for only a few minutes. Sometimes the territory is just for one animal; in other cases it may be for a pair, a family group, or for an entire herd or swarm.

Holding a territory
Territories are defended in various ways. Animals may proclaim their ownership and warn others to stay away using the bright colours and patterns of their bodies. They may make loud calls or powerful smells, or perform intricate dances and other displays. This book looks at why animals have territories, the many kinds of territories that occur in nature, and the ways in which animals obtain and keep their own patch of land so that they can survive in the competitive natural world.

Male topi in Kenya tussle for a territory, but neither animal is likely to be injured in the confrontation.

WHY HAVE TERRITORIES?

An animal's territory is the space which helps it to survive. The territory may provide food, a place to mate and raise young, or a safe site to rest.

A tiger sprays smelly urine on the grass to mark the edge of his jungle territory.

Not all animals are territorial. But those that are may fight aggressively to obtain or defend their territory – occasionally to the death. Some animals have large territories which contain all the food they need. Other territories are only large enough to rest or breed in.

Food for the big cats

A pride (group) of lions preys on the zebras, antelopes and other animals of the African savanna. The pride has a territory which must contain enough prey animals to feed all its members, including the cubs. The territory may be up to 400 square kilometres in size. Pride members have different duties. The females do most of the hunting. The males defend the pride's territory. They leave urine and droppings around its edges, patrol the boundary and roar threateningly at outsiders.

In India, tigers also have territories, but they do not live in groups. Each tiger has its own territory, which it patrols and defends against other tigers. The territory must contain enough animals that can be easily caught to feed the tiger. This predator also needs suitable trees for resting in, and pools in which to drink and cool off with a swim. An average tiger territory is about 50 square kilometres. As the trees are felled by people, the jungle gets smaller, and there are less territories for tigers.

A number of tiger territories are shown here in dark green. In rocky and hilly places, where the jungle is less productive, tigers need bigger territories.

Lionesses doze after a hunt. The male is away patrolling the pride's territory.

A nest-site for breeding birds

Many seabirds nest on cliff ledges. The best ledges, with enough room for a nest and a place to perch out of reach of hunters, are usually in short supply. Gannets, guillemots and razorbills form huge, noisy colonies on cliffs in the breeding season. Each breeding pair of birds vigorously defend their own nest-ledge. Crowding helps to protect all the eggs and chicks from predators such as gulls. To avoid out-and-out fighting, cliff-nesting birds have a complicated code of calls and body movements, that warn others in the colony to keep off their territory (see pages 22-3).

Most species of birds nest and lay their eggs in spring. At this time they often become territorial. While the female blackbird looks after the nest, the male defends his family and territory from any threat. He needs enough garden or hedgerow to provide sufficient insects and grubs to feed the family. He sings loudly to warn others to keep away, and chases off any blackbirds that ignore his warning.

A roost for resting starlings

Starlings usually live in large groups. Every morning they fly out to the fields in huge flocks to feed. They return in the evening to their night-time roosts in trees or on building ledges.

There may be more than a million birds in a large flock of starlings. Each bird needs a sheltered spot to rest during the night. So it squabbles and pushes to squeeze itself onto a perch between the other birds. The nearer it gets to the middle of the flock, the safer it is, so these perches are fought over the most. Each perch is a particular bird's resting territory for the night.

Starlings roost in large flocks, and squabble with one another to establish a good perch.

A gannet approaches the nest. These seabirds defend their tiny cliff-top territories by pecking at each other and wrestling with their beaks. Only rarely do their mock fights get out of control and cause injury.

DEFENDING A TERRITORY

Animals need to protect their precious territories, mainly from others of their own species. To frighten off intruders they advertise their ownership by a variety of visual displays, sounds and smells.

Many territory-owners defend their territories only against others of their own species. This is because animals from the same species are the most likely to eat the same kinds of food, and need the same type of sheltering place. This means direct competition. Creatures from different species generally have different needs, so they can live side by side in the same area without too much interference or competition from each other.

Defence by fighting consumes large amounts of energy and could result in injury, or even death. So animals have developed all sorts of ways of proclaiming their ownership of a territory and scaring away intruders, without having to fight. They use colourful displays, smells, songs and roars to get their message across.

See and be seen

Many animals, especially birds and fish, send visual messages with their brightly coloured bodies. They may use special movements to show off their colours. The kingfisher has shining blue-and-orange colours which are unmistakable. Each pair of birds has a territory along a stretch of river. Their plumage is so distinctive that they do not need to display it in a special way. The birds have only to fly along the river bank as they feed, and their presence is obvious to any intruding kingfishers. The bright colours also warn predators which might eat them that the flesh of the kingfisher tastes horrible!

The shy kingfisher is a territorial bird. It must catch enough fish every day to feed itself, and needs a suitable river bank in which to dig a nest tunnel. It cannot afford to let other kingfishers live on its part of the river.

No room for manoeuvre

In a small aquarium, the famous male Siamese fightingfish will fight each other savagely. This may be because the aquarium is too small to allow each male to set up his own territory. In the wild these fishes usually only display to each other until one retreats. Although he is very aggressive, the male fightingfish is a caring father. In the breeding season he defends a territory where he keeps his eggs in a bubble nest.

Sniffing the still night air, a common shrew listens out for trespassers in its territory.

Male Siamese fightingfish warn each other to retreat by making their shiny colours even brighter, and by swimming around each other, waving their fins and flapping their gill covers. Occasionally a fight breaks out. The fish may lock jaws, and bite each other's fins and scales.

Sounding a warning

Sound offers another good way of communicating. Humans tend to rely on eyesight. But many animals have a much keener sense of hearing than we do, and can detect much fainter sounds. These sounds may be important in marking the boundaries of a territory and telling outsiders to keep away.

The tiny shrew is a solitary animal that feeds on insects and worms. It warns other shrews to keep away from its feeding territory with a series of high-pitched screams. A challenger can judge the strength of his opponent from the pitch and loudness of the screams.

The robin is a fiercely territorial bird. Its red breast acts as a warning sign to others of its species. A robin will approach and threaten any small red object which appears in its territory. To let other robins know the territory is occupied, a robin may sing from a high perch at any point during the day. Singing means he or she does not have to continually chase away intruders.

MESSAGES AT A DISTANCE

Colourful displays and small sounds are limited. They can only be seen and heard by others nearby. When a creature needs to advertise its territory ownership over a greater distance, loud calls and lingering smells may be much more effective.

Forest calls

It is very difficult to see far in a dense forest. But loud sounds travel well through the trees, to broadcast a message that can be heard far and wide.

One of the loudest sounds in the rainforests of Southeast Asia is the call of the siamang. These large gibbons live high in the treetops in family groups, usually consisting of a mother, father and young. They sing together to communicate to other families that the area is occupied. The siamang's whooping call is amplified (made louder) by its balloon-like throat sac, and can be heard a kilometre away.

The great spotted woodpecker hammers at a treetrunk to produce a loud burst of sound.

A female siamang calls loudly to communicate with her family and to warn off rivals.

Rhinos are short-sighted, and much of their behaviour is stimulated by the odours of urine and faeces. Horn-waving between rival males occurs only if smell signals left to mark territory are ignored.

There are over 200 species of woodpeckers. Most kinds are territorial. Each bird needs an area of forest large enough to provide the insects and wood-boring grubs it feeds on. The woodpecker signals its ownership of a patch of forest by "drumming", rapidly striking a hollow tree with its beak. The hollow tree makes the sounds louder so they echo across the forest.

Signalling with smells

Scents can be very powerful signals. Many animals defend their territory by leaving smelly dung or urine round the borders, to warn off intruders. Smells last a long time, often many days. They are very distinctive and can keep sending the message long after the animals that left them have moved on.

Rhinos are solitary animals that live alone, with the exception of a mother bringing up young. Each rhino has a large home range, which provides all the plant food and water it needs. A female rhino does not mind if her home range overlaps with the ranges of other females. But male rhinos are very territorial, and defend their home ranges fiercely. The boundaries of each territory are marked with large piles of dung. When two males meet, they perform a complicated ritual. They stare at each other, wipe their horns on the ground and spray urine backwards.

Smells can also be posted in other ways. Some kinds of deer have scent glands between their toes and just in front of their eyes. Males use the smelly secretions from these glands to mark trees, warning rivals away.

Keeping the group together

Some foxes live in groups of one male and two or three females. They eat small mammals, worms, insects and plant material such as fruit. The group defends its territory by carefully placing urine and droppings around it. This keeps the group together and warns other foxes to stay away.

A red fox vixen marks her territory with the individual odour of her urine.

African hunting dogs live in packs and hunt gazelle, wildebeest and zebra on the savanna. The pack has no home, unless there are pups to look after. But it does have a territory. Like pet dogs, hunting dogs communicate largely by smell. The scent of their droppings and urine helps members of the pack to keep together, and prevents other packs from coming too close.

FINDING ENOUGH FOOD

Animals need enough food to stay healthy and rear a family. Many animal territories are used to provide this food. The size of the territory depends on the size of the animal, what sort of food it eats, and how plentiful the food is in the particular area.

In general, carnivores (meat-eaters) need a larger area of land to support them than do herbivores (plant-eaters). A herbivore's territory must be big enough to contain the plants it needs to provide it with energy. Carnivores prey on herbivores (and smaller or weaker carnivores), so a carnivore's territory must be larger and hold enough animals to sustain it.

Territory size also depends on other factors. A large animal which eats a very specialised kind of food, and lives in a harsh habitat such as polar ice, may need a territory of hundreds of square kilometres to keep it going. A smaller creature in a food-rich place like a rainforest or a coral reef may need only a few square metres.

Large territories
Animals that live in harsh conditions such as frozen tundra or dry desert usually need very large territories to survive. They generally live alone.

The snow leopard inhabits the mountains of the Himalayas. There is little vegetation at such heights, so few plant-eating animals live there. This means the snow leopard's prey is scarce. It eats mountain goats, ibex, boars and some birds. It needs a vast area, up to 100 square kilometres, to supply it with enough meat for survival.

The main food of the giant panda, from China, is a type of bamboo. It needs to eat huge amounts, because bamboo is woody and tough, difficult to digest, and not very nourishing. Pandas live alone, each one in a territory of up to seven square kilometres – a very large area for a solitary herbivore.

The snow leopard from Asia is carnivorous, and searches for prey among mountain rocks.

Giant pandas are herbivores. They have become very rare as their forest territories are cut down.

The dragonfly patrols its riverside or lakeside territory, flashing in the summer sun. These large, active insects hunt great quantities of smaller insects to keep them going. They have relatively big territories which they defend aggressively, and they are very curious about any other animals in their patch. They will even fly close to humans to check that they are not a threat.

The hawker dragonfly's huge eyes scan for prey – and for intruders in its territory.

The African golden-winged sunbird feeds only on nectar from certain flowers. It needs 1,600 of these flowers within its territory to provide it with enough food. The size of the sunbird's territory depends on how many plants it contains, and how many are in flower at any one time.

Small territories

If food is abundant, or if an animal can eat a very varied diet, its territory is more likely to be small, or almost non-existent. Sea anemones catch and sting small fish and other creatures which swim nearby. This food is quite plentiful, so anemones need only enough space to attach themselves to a rock. But they will defend this tiny territory against other sea anemones. The resident anemone bends towards an intruder and stings with its tentacles until the intruder shuffles off.

Sea anemones slide slowly over rocks to find a spot where food is easy to catch. An anemone already in a good position will fend off rivals by stinging them.

A PLACE TO REST

Not all animals use their territories to provide food. Some simply have them as a place to rest. A territory used for this purpose, often called a roost, may be only a small area around the animal.

Personal space

Most animals function best if they are not overcrowded. They have a "personal territory", which in some species is very small. But it is still defended like a larger territory, and trespassers provoke an aggressive response.

A small personal territory has advantages. It makes it easier for animals that live communally to keep in touch about food, breeding and overcrowding, if they are near to each other.

Pipistrelle bats prefer to live in large colonies. They have hardly any personal space as they roost together in the roofs of old barns or in church towers, tightly packed to keep warm. Bats are nocturnal (active at night). When it is dark they fly out to feed on insects. During their daytime roost, each member of the colony keeps in touch with its neighbours using squeaks and smells. However, when the babies are born, the females find resting sites away from the males, and rear the young there.

Male budgerigars try to out-stare each other for the most desirable perch in their night-time roost.

When darkness falls, pipistrelle bats leave the crowded roost for their nightly feeding flight.

No fixed abode

Some animals spend life constantly on the move in search of food, and establish a new territory to rest in each night. Budgerigars came originally from Australia, although they are now familiar round the world as cage birds. These small parrots live mainly on grass seeds, which they search for in large flocks. Flock members need to keep in touch with each other because the flock is constantly moving to new feeding grounds. Every night they find a tree to roost in. The birds squabble and chatter to find and keep a perch. They have no fixed breeding season; they nest and rear young whenever there is plenty of food.

Safety in numbers

Vulnerable animals often live in large groups for protection. A big group of small creatures may frighten off or confuse a predator. Even if it does not, the predator can only capture one or a few prey at a time.

Mackerel live in huge shoals in the surface waters of the Atlantic Ocean. They migrate around the Atlantic throughout the year, spawning in summer in shallower waters near northern shores. Each mackerel has about the same personal space, so that the whole shoal is evenly spaced out. With each member at the same distance from its neighbours, the shoal is able to wheel and turn as though it were one huge animal. This could frighten away potential hunters.

Population control

For certain kinds of creatures which live in groups, a sense of personal territory can work communally as a form of population control. This can help to prevent the colony from getting too big and using up all its food, which would cause mass starvation. As overcrowding increases, group members become more aggressive towards each other, and they do not breed so well. The numbers are then reduced.

Many kinds of rats, mice and other rodents react to overpopulation in this way. Lemmings from northern Europe become easily irritated and squabble more as their numbers rise and they become too crowded. Eventually they form bands and set off in search of a new area with plenty of space and food. As they march they may get funnelled by the landscape into a valley or ravine leading into a river or over a cliff. So strong is their urge to find a new home that they do not stop, and thousands may perish in these marches.

Swimming in surface waters, individual mackerel are difficult to pick out from the shoal.

After years of plentiful food, the lemming population can become so large that food grows scarce. What seems like a suicide march is really a search for a less crowded area, where food is abundant again.

GROUP TERRITORY

Territories may belong to a single animal, a pair or a group. Some kinds of animals survive best alone, while others do well in huge colonies. The type of territory is closely linked to group size.

Loners

Some kinds of animals live solitary lives. Individuals occupy territories and never allow others to enter. The only exception to this is at breeding time.

An example is the European river bullhead, which lives alone in its own stretch of river. In spring the male fish makes a nest and briefly allows the female to approach and lay her eggs. He then drives her away, and guards the eggs until they hatch. When the young grow, he chases them away, too. For the rest of the year he allows no other bullheads in his territory.

Pairs

Many animals live in pairs. Some pair for life (see page 21), others only while they are raising young.

Beavers pair for life, and together the male and female build a dam, and make a home called a lodge. They have two or more offspring every spring, and allow the young to stay with them in the lodge for about two years. Then territorial behaviour takes over from parental behaviour. The parents drive the young away. Each youngster must find an unoccupied area or take over a territory, to start a colony of its own.

With its underwater entrance, the beavers' lodge provides a safe home for the whole family. In the deep pool created by the dam, green wood can be stored for winter food.

A male bullhead protects his eggs from other fish, and his territory from other bullheads.

Extended families

Some animals live in extended families. In such groups, youngsters are allowed to stay with their parents, even when they become adults. Young adults help their parents to raise more offspring.

Gorillas and chimpanzees live in extended families. Groups of gorillas usually have only one senior male, but there may be two or more chief females. Their young are allowed to stay in the group until they become a threat. Then they must leave the family home. The troop's home range is up to 20 square kilometres in area, and the ranges of neighbouring troops overlap. If rival males meet, they threaten each other by beating their chests, roaring, tearing down twigs and rushing sideways.

Female gorillas and young are defended by the troop's large "silverback" male.

Harems

A group known as a "harem" consists of many females with one dominant male. In some species of animals the harem grouping lasts all year, in other species it operates only in the breeding season. Horses, deer, seals and sea-lions, such as the Californian sea-lion, group themselves in this way. The average bull (mature male) Californian sea-lion has a harem of 10-20 cows (females).

In harem groups, the male must be strong and healthy, since he has to defend the females (and often their young) from rival males and from predators. His offspring are likely to inherit his features and grow up strong and healthy, too.

Matriarchies

Some kinds of animals live in groups where the females are dominant. Elephants are an example. Each elephant herd is controlled by a dominant older female, the matriarch. She lives with her daughters and their offspring, and they all co-operate in raising the young. Males live alone or in small bachelor groups, and are only allowed near the females for mating.

A matriarchal group of African cow elephants and calves bathe and quench their thirst.

STAGE SHOW

Many male animals show off to females as part of their breeding behaviour. They establish a small, special territory where they display their colourful plumage or large antlers, their great strength or dancing abilities.

In many animal species, breeding is a testing time for males eager to take part in mating. Each male competes with others to prove himself the best, so that he will be chosen by as many females as possible as their mate.

In order to show themselves to best advantage, many male animals – and females in a few species – have territories which they use solely for displaying themselves. These territories have no value for feeding or bringing up young. But they are a symbol of success and proof of the owner's prowess.

Leks

A territory used only for breeding display is known as a lek. It must be exactly right for the performance. It is usually quite small, and there are often several leks together in one site. The best leks are always fiercely fought over and vigorously defended, because success at getting a good lek means that the occupier is more likely to mate.

Several kinds of birds and a few mammals use leks for display. Females are attracted to the lek area, called the leking ground, by the calls of the males. The females stand around the edges, watching the performances and choosing the best male to father their young. Males with leks usually mate with as many females as they can, but take no interest in the babies afterwards.

In the brushland of North America, male sage grouse gather at the same leking grounds every year. These are areas of scrub worn bare by many years of dancing feet. Sage grouse are the largest North American grouse, each bird weighing up to four kilograms. The males display and fight, and the top birds get the best leks.

In a blur of feathers, male sage grouse battle for a good display area, or lek.

Once the leks are won, the male grouse begin their spectacular mating displays. They raise their tail feathers and puff out their breasts, rattling the feathers as they make bubbling calls. They show off the yellow-orange inflatable patches on their necks, and finish the show with a cracking sound. The females select the males with the most impressive displays and the best leks as the fathers for their young.

A male great bowerbird tidies his avenue-like bower and its decorations.

The leks of the male grouse are clearly defined. Once each bird has claimed a lek it dances and calls to attract females. This also warns off challengers and so limits any real fighting.

Beautiful bowers

The bowerbirds of Australia also use leks in the breeding season. Once the male has won a lek site, he spends much of his time there making and decorating a bower. This is a special structure built for the purpose of attracting as many female birds as possible for mating.

The different bowerbird species build four main types of bower: mats, avenues, towers, and complex hut-like structures. The bowers are made of twigs and decorated with colourful objects such as flowers, feathers and fruits. Some birds even paint their bowers with sap or fruit juice! The male and female birds mate at the bower. Then the female leaves to build a nest and raise the young alone.

Starved off the lek

Leking behaviour has also been discovered in the hartebeest of Africa. The males fight for a good lek site – the best are at the centre of the area, where the females congregate. Here the males strut to and fro, attracting as many females as they can. Once they have taken possession of a site, they must stay and defend it, even though the small, bare patch provides hardly any food. The males get thinner and hungrier as the breeding season continues, until they give up their sites to fitter animals.

Outside the breeding season, hartebeest live together in peaceful groups.

SUPPORTING A FAMILY

Animals need extra food and protection when they are raising a family. Many animals that are not territorial for the rest of the year establish a territory at this time.

The nightingale is one of the few woodland birds that sings throughout the day.

Spring in the air
In Europe and North America, most animals breed in spring and early summer. The weather becomes warmer, the days get longer, plants grow faster, and small animals hatch or come out of hibernation. Food is more plentiful, and it is an ideal time to rear young.

The "keep out" song
During the breeding season parents use up more energy than usual, building a nest or shelter and caring for their offspring. The young eat more and more food as they grow. Many animals have territories only during this time, to make sure they have a suitable nest site and enough food for their offspring.

In Britain, the nightingale's beautiful song is heard from May onwards. It sings all day, and part of the night too, to make sure others do not trespass onto its territory. The nightingale parent must find enough worms and insects to feed four or five young. A dull brown bird that hides in bushes, it is well camouflaged from predators, but uses its song to warn off others of its species.

Family duties
Many kinds of animals pair up not only to mate, but to rear their offspring as well. They defend the nest site and feed the young together. In other species, the male mates with several females, who then bring up their young alone.

Jewel cichlids are fish of tropical lakes. Both male and female are conscientious parents. The female sticks her eggs to the surface of a rock, a territory which both parents have cleaned thoroughly. They fan the eggs to prevent parasites and fungal growth from infesting them. When the babies hatch, the parents carry them in their mouths to a nest hollow in the gravel. Any young that stray are quickly returned to the nest. When the offspring are big enough, the parents escort them on practice swims, keeping them together in a tight shoal. All through this time, both parents vigorously defend their territory, chasing off intruders.

Jewel cichlids fan their clutch of eggs to keep them clean until they hatch.

Golden eagles pair for life, and split family duties between them. They use the same nest site every year, and defend a large territory of up to 40 square kilometres around it, which provides enough hares and grouse to feed their chicks. The male does most of the hunting, bringing food back to his family. The female stays at the nest, known as an eyrie, tending the young.

Spotted sandpipers squabble at the breeding ground. Each female has more than one male in her territory, but one of the males is senior and will try to drive off the other fathers.

Male mothers

The male stickleback defends and provides for his young. In spring this fish develops a bright red underside, chooses a territory and drives off other males of his kind. Like the robin (see page 9), he attacks anything red. He builds a tunnel nest and entices a female to lay her eggs in it. He then drives her off too, and tends the young alone.

A male three-spined stickleback will chase away the female after she has laid her eggs.

Role reversal

Spotted sandpipers have unusual parental roles, compared to most animals. The females divide up the breeding grounds into territories, then each one defends her own patch aggressively. A female attracts a male to her territory and lays her eggs in his nest. She leaves him to incubate them and feed the young while she goes courting again. Meanwhile, she continues to forage for food and defend her territory against other females.

BOUNDARY CONFRONTATION

Territorial disputes do not normally involve fighting, which would leave opponents weak or injured. Most territorial animals have complex displays involving body postures and movements, which are understood by the rivals, and which help to prevent injury.

The colours of the male mandrill's face highlight the various expressions he makes.

Facial expressions

The male mandrill has one of the most colourful of all animal faces. Like other monkeys, mandrills live in highly organised groups. They use a variety of facial expressions to communicate with others in their group. When a mandrill "snarls", it is in fact making a friendly gesture to a member of its troop. When it "yawns", it is warning members of another troop to keep away. Other monkeys and apes use facial expressions – including ourselves.

The way an animal behaves at its territory's boundary is very revealing. Often, it has an "ownership display" which it performs best and most completely at the centre of its territory. The performance gets less confident and more fragmented as the animal approaches the centre of the territory next door. This changing behaviour results in an invisible line or boundary, where neighbouring territory-holders perform with equal intensity. In some kinds of animals, the performance of movements and gestures is enough to warn off intruders. In other species the display involves a mock fight. Real fighting only occurs if all warning signals are ignored.

The threat posture in guillemots, shown in (1) by the bird on the right, is aimed at intimidating an opponent and causing it to retreat. If a fight seems likely, it may be averted by one of several appeasement postures. These are exaggerated movements such as side-preening (2), stretching away from the other bird (3), or bowing with outstretched wings (4).

Guillemot colonies are very dense – more than 50 pairs of birds per square metre.

Lorikeets are small parrots from the Tropics whose favourite food is nectar and pollen from blossom. When a tree comes into blossom, members of the flock compete for the nectar. Each bird aggressively defends its own patch of flowers with a combination of fluttering, scratching, bobbing, bouncing and hissing. The birds' gaudy feathers make this display even more impressive.

Solving disputes by dancing

The crowded guillemot colony on the cliff face is made up of thousands of tiny territories, each just large enough for a pair of birds to incubate one egg. In this precarious society, fighting would result in eggs and injured birds falling into the sea. So neighbours have two main types of behaviour to keep order. One is the threat display, through which a bird warns an opponent that a fight is imminent unless the opponent backs down. The other is a gesture of appeasement or submission, through which a bird signals that it is backing down or giving in. In guillemots, submission gestures include feather preening and a stiff-legged bowing walk.

Red-flanked lorikeets will jostle for territory in a blossom-laden tree.

BIGGEST AND BEST-ARMED

Territorial displays, like breeding displays, often emphasise the size of an animal, or show off its weapons, to intimidate and frighten an opponent.

Acting big
The frilled lizard of Australia is only about 70 centimetres long, and most of this length is tail. However, it can make itself look much bigger by raising the frill or collar of skin around its neck. The collar is brightly coloured, and the lizard gapes wide its mouth at the same time. This display is usually enough to frighten off other lizards – and most predators, as well.

The frilled lizard's frightening display is mostly bluff. If it fails to scare an intruder, the lizard will climb the nearest tree to safety.

Puffed feathers and fur
Many birds fluff out their feathers to keep warm. Mammals do the same with their fur. This technique also makes the animal seem larger, and shows off colourful feathers or fur to best advantage. It is often included in threat displays, against territorial intruders and possible predators.

Like wild dogs, a pet dog is territorial. It defends its owner's house from intruders by barking, accompanied by the threat display of "raising its hackles". The hair along the dog's back stands on end, making the animal appear larger than it is.

The black bear is another animal that tries to appear bigger as part of its threat display. This solitary animal eats mainly fruit, nuts and honey, and some small animals. When disturbed, it rears up to its full two-metre height and opens wide its arms, to reveal the white patch on its chest for an added element of surprise.

Lethal weapons
In the wild, a stallion (male horse) has several females in his herd. He spends most of his time attracting other females, and defending the herd against predators and other stallions who stray into the area. His threat display includes arching his neck and doing a slow, bouncy trot that makes him look bigger. The trot also shows off his main weapons – his hooves. If this display fails, he will fight viciously, biting and kicking an opponent.

The huge antlers of the male moose of North America are the largest of any deer. Moose live alone, feeding on leaves, twigs and water plants. To threaten another moose intruding on his territory, the bull (male) will toss his head and show off his great antlers. If it comes to a fight, the flat antlers rarely cause injury. Exhaustion usually decides between winner and loser.

The trot of an Arabian stallion aims to impress mares and any rival stallions nearby.

The bull moose's antlers look impressive, but they are heavy and awkward to use as weapons.

The male African warthog's main weapons are the fearsome tusks which protrude from his mouth. Attention is drawn to them by lumpy growths, the "warts" all over his face, which make him look even more ferocious. The tusks and warts are less obvious in the female. The warthog is a fierce animal which does not tolerate intruders, including humans, in its territory.

A strong and sturdy animal, the male warthog is up to two metres in length, including his tail. His warts are fleshy lumps and knobs, and his tusks are overgrown canine teeth which can be 60 centimetres long.

RITUAL FIGHTING

When animals confront one another over territory ownership, they often look as if they are fighting. But many species go through the motions of a fight without actually touching or even coming near each other. This type of activity is called ritualised behaviour.

Wolves live in packs with a strict hierarchy, enforced by ritual gestures of threat and appeasement.

Ritualised behaviour is behaviour which has become separate from its original purpose, from feeding to fighting, and is used instead for a different purpose. Many animal species have ritual motions and postures which all members recognise. Ritual fighting is used for territorial defence, but prevents real violence and injury from occurring.

Many animals have fearsome-looking weapons, such as antlers or teeth, which are shown off in ritual threat displays. These weapons may be so large that although they look good, in a real fight they are too big to be effective.

Butting battles

Male goats and sheep use their horns to defend themselves and their mates from other males, and from predators such as big cats. These animals fight by butting each other. Butting looks dangerous, but mainly tests the strength and endurance of the two animals, and is unlikely to inflict injury. The goats' horns, skull, backbone and muscles are able to absorb most of the shocks and knocks of repeated butting. The stronger animal with the greatest stamina wins the contest, usually without any real damage being done to either creature.

In the breeding season, bighorn rams lean on each other in a pre-fight show of strength.

During the rutting season, when mating takes place, red deer stags battle to keep their females. They roar and strut in front of each other, and sometimes this display is enough to decide the contest. If not, the stags face each other, lock antlers and push. This pushing contest rarely causes serious injury to either animal. The winner is the stag that pushes the other off the site.

| Thoughtful | Annoyed |
| Curious | Pleased |

King of the castle

The male African antelopes called topi are very territorial (see page 5). Male topi have leks, and each animal marks his patch of ground with dung and scent rubbings. The topi stands with his front feet on a termite mound, so that his head is raised above those around him. When another male approaches, he lowers his head and points his horns at the intruder, who does the same. The two animals drop to their knees and stay there, confronting each other but not touching, until one backs off.

Male fallow deer are more likely to exhaust themselves than sustain injury.

A threatening smile

Chimpanzees live in highly organised troops. The more senior, or dominant, animals regularly threaten the junior ones by baring their teeth, producing an expression which looks to us like a smile. The juniors respond with gestures of submission, hiding their teeth and crouching or flattening themselves against the ground, so that they appear as small as possible.

These gestures also occur when one troop strays into another's area. All the resident adults show threatening behaviour, while the intruders submit.

Chimps use facial expressions to communicate their mood to others in their group, or to intruders. Humans sometimes make the mistake of assuming that chimps' expressions carry the same meaning as our own.

THE BIG FIGHT

When ritual displays and warnings fail, a real fight may occur. Most animals that are likely to fight have protection, such as thick wads of fat or tough hair, to reduce the risk of permanent damage. Strong, young animals usually recover, but the old and sick have less chance of winning, or even surviving.

Male southern elephant seals mock-fight as the breeding season begins.

In most species of animals, serious fighting only happens if conditions are bad, due to overcrowding or lack of food or water. This is true of territorial behaviour, too. If there is not enough room for all the animals concerned to have a territory, the chances of a real fight developing are higher.

Southern elephant seals live in the South Atlantic and Pacific Oceans, and are able to breed on the beaches of only a few islands there. The huge males fight viciously for a beach territory where they can keep their harem of females. Each male threatens the others by roaring and inflating his nose, but often this display does not prevent battle. In a fight, two males rear up and lunge at each other's necks with their long canine teeth. The necks are padded with protective fat, but wounds soon occur.

The strongest male wins control of the territory and becomes "beachmaster". But as soon as his strength begins to fail, often as a result of his injuries, there are many others waiting to take over.

Bitten to death

Hippos are very territorial animals. A male hippo fiercely defends the stretch of river where his females and their young live. Opposing males display to one another, opening their mouths wide to show off huge canine teeth, and spraying their droppings.

Occasionally fights break out, and these can last for more than an hour. The canine teeth are up to 50 centimetres long and make excellent weapons. Although the hippo's skin is thick and tough, and heals quickly, wounds can sometimes be fatal.

Hippos roar and spar over territory along a stretch of river in Tanzania.

Arms and legs

Kangaroos have sharp claws and very powerful back legs and tails. When fighting over mates or territory, kangaroos box and wrestle with one another. Each male uses his front paws to manoeuvre himself into a position where he can balance himself on his tail and kick his opponent with both feet. A well-aimed kick with his sharp foot claws can damage a rival's internal organs and may result in serious injury.

Defending to the death

Bees and some wasps labour to feed and house their queen, themselves and their sisters. They cannot survive without the nest which contains their food store and their queen. They defend this territory to the death, stinging any other animal that comes too close. When a bee stings, its body is damaged so much that it dies. Wasps can usually sting several times before the action of stinging kills them.

A paper-wasp from Greece makes a nest of cells for the eggs from chewed-up wood.

As scientists continue their research, they discover new examples of animal territories, and learn more about the kinds of behaviour associated with them. Such research can only be done properly in wild, unspoilt areas, since animals confined in zoos or in unfamiliar surroundings may not behave naturally. This research may help us to understand more about the behaviour of one very important animal indeed – the human.

Adult kangaroos are over two metres tall, and are very strong. In a contest they can inflict great injury if one does not back down. Mainly males fight, over females and grazing sites for their family group.

SPOT IT YOURSELF

You can study animals and the way they behave almost anywhere. Learn to detect animals by the signs they leave: burrow entrances, nests, footprints in mud or snow, hair caught in wire or branches, droppings, half-eaten leaves and discarded shells. Approach creatures downwind, so your scent does not give you away. When nature-spotting, keep as still and quiet as possible.

Practical tips for nature-spotting
Wear wind- and water- proof clothing in dull colours. Polaroid glasses reduce surface reflection for seeing underwater. A lens magnifies small animals and a camping mat gives some comfort.

Foxes patrol the boundaries of fields and meadows.

Shrews hunt worms in their hedgerow territories.

A robin sings in its patch of woodland.

A blackbird bows and flaps at an intruder.

An otter leaves droppings to mark its section of riverbank.

Owls keep watch at dusk from nest holes high in trees.

Take a notebook and pencil with you to record your finds outside. A pocket field guide will help you to identify animals.

Take care of nature
When studying animals in natural surroundings, make notes and take photos, but don't capture or frighten creatures. They will behave unnaturally in captivity, or if you disturb them. Take all your litter home with you, and follow the local wildlife laws.

GLOSSARY

Behaviour The actions and movements of an animal, including sleeping, feeding and courting.

Camouflage The disguise through which an animal imitates part of its surroundings or another object.

Carnivore An animal that eats mainly meat.

Courtship behaviour The actions of an animal when it is trying to attract a mate.

Harem A breeding group in which one male mates with and dominates several females.

Herbivore An animal that eats mainly plant material such as leaves, stems, roots or fruit.

Instinctive An action or behaviour which is "built in" from birth, and does not have to be learned.

Lek A small patch of land which animals of one sex (usually males) fight over, because ownership means a greater chance of success in attracting and mating with members of the other sex.

Lodge The mound-shaped home of a beaver family, built in a lake.

Matriarch The female leader of an animal group, such as the experienced cow elephant who leads her herd.

Predator An animal that hunts other creatures for food.

Prey An animal hunted for food by a predator.

Ritual behaviour Behaviour which has become separated from its original purpose, and is used for another purpose. For example, rival male birds may threaten each other for a territory by making exaggerated feeding movements.

Roost A place where an animal such as a bird or bat rests or sleeps in relative safety.

Rutting Behaviour of male deer in the breeding season, when they roar and tussle with each other, competing for control of females in the herd.

Spawn Newly-laid eggs, usually of water creatures such as fish or frogs.

Species A group of living things with the same characteristics, that can breed together.

Submission posture A body posture through which an animal signals that it is submitting or "giving in" to a senior member of its group. This is similar to an appeasement gesture.

Territory A patch of land or other area claimed by an animal and defended against others, usually of its own kind. Its defensive actions are called territorial behaviour.

Threat display Behaviour which shows off the size, colours, patterns, or weapons of an animal, in an attempt to intimidate rivals or frighten them away.

Warning coloration The distinctive colours and patterns of an animal's skin which warn that it is poisonous or tastes horrible.

INDEX

antelopes 6, 27
antlers 18, 25, 26, 27
apes 22
appeasement gestures 23, 26, 31

bats 14, 31
bear, black 24
beavers 16, 31
bees 29
bird song 7, 9, 20
blackbird 7, 30
boar 12
bowerbird 19
breeding behaviour 18-19, 24
breeding season 7, 9, 14, 19, 20, 28, 31
budgerigars 14
bullhead 16

camouflage 20
carnivores 12, 31
chimpanzees 17, 27
cichlid fish 20
colour displays 10
colours 5, 8, 21, 22, 24, 31
courtship 31

deer 11, 17, 27, 31
displays 5, 8, 9, 10, 18, 22, 23, 24
dogs 11, 24
dragonfly 13
droppings 6, 11, 27, 28, 30

eagles, golden 21
elephants 17, 31
eyrie 21

facial expressions 22, 27
family groups 17
feeding 31
fightingfish 9
fish 8, 15, 16, 20, 31
flowers 13, 23
foxes 11, 30
frogs 31

gannets 7
gazelles 11
giant panda 12
gibbons 10
goats 12, 26
gorillas 17
grouse 18, 19, 21
guillemots 7, 23
gulls 7

harem 17, 31
hartebeest 19
herbivores 12, 31
hibernation 20
hierarchy 26
hippos 28
horses 17, 24, 25
humans 9, 13, 25, 29
hunting dog 11

kangaroos 29
kingfisher 8

leks 18-19, 27, 31
lemmings 15
leopard, snow 12
lions 6
lizard, frilled 24
lodge 16, 31
lorikeets 23

mackerel 15
mammals 11, 18, 24
mandrill 22
matriarch 17, 31
mice 15
monkeys 22
moose 25

nectar 13, 23
nightingale 20

otter 30
owl 30
ownership display 22

personal territory 14-15
predators 6, 7, 8, 15, 17, 20, 24, 26, 31
prey 6, 12, 13, 15, 31

rabbits 21
rats 15
razorbills 7
rhinos 10, 11
ritual behaviour 11, 26, 28, 31
robin 9, 21, 30
roosts 7, 14, 31
rutting 27, 31

sandpipers 21
scents 11, 27, 30
sea anemones 13
sea-lions 17
seals 17, 28
sheep 26, 27
shrews 9, 30
siamang 10
smells 5, 8, 10-11, 14
snow leopard 12
sounds 8, 9, 10
starlings 7
stickleback 21
submission 23, 27, 31
sunbird 13

territorial behaviour 5, 16, 22, 24, 28, 31
threat displays 17, 23, 24, 26, 27, 31
tiger 6
topi 5, 27

urine 6, 10, 11

warning coloration 31
warthog 25
wasps 29
weapons 24, 25, 26, 28, 31
wild dogs 24
wildebeest 11
wolves 26
woodpeckers 10

zebras 6, 11

32